THE POWER OF SMART MONEY MANAGEMENT: How to live well on a budget and invest wisely for your future

Debbie Emerald

Copyright © 2023 by Debbie Emerald "The Power of Smart Money Management". All rights reserved. No part of this publication may be reproduced, distributed, or transmitted in any form or by any means, including photocopying, recording, or other electronic or mechanical methods, without the prior written permission of the publisher, except in the case of brief quotations embodied in critical reviews and certain other noncommercial uses permitted by copyright law. For permission requests, write to the publisher, addressed;peculiaremerald02@gmail.com.

TABLE OF CONTENTS

INTRODUCTION

CHAPTER ONE: SETTING UP YOUR BUDGET
1.1. UNDERSTANDING YOUR FINANCIAL SITUATION
1.2. ESTABLISHING FINANCIAL GOALS
1.3. CREATING A BUDGET
1.4. TRACKING YOUR EXPENSES
CHAPTER TWO: STICKING TO A BUDGET
2.1. UNDERSTANDING SELF-CONTROL AND SELF-IMPOSED LIMIT
2.2 MAKING A SMART CHOICE

2.3 AVOIDING UNNECESSARY SPENDING
2.4 DON'T GIVE UP
CHAPTER THREE: INVEST WISELY
3.1. EVALUATING INVESTMENT OPPORTUNITIES
3.2 AVOIDING SCAM
3.3. CREATING A PORTFOLIO
3.4. DIVERSIFYING YOUR INVESTMENT

CONCLUSION

INTRODUCTION

THE SMART MONEY CONCEPT

Smart money is a financial concept that focuses on making smart decisions with money. It is about using resources responsibly and wisely and making decisions that can benefit both you and your finances in the long run.

Smart money decisions involve choosing investments that have higher risk but higher rewards, as well as prioritizing debt repayment and saving for the future.

Smart money management also means considering the big picture looking at the overall financial picture and how the different pieces of it interact. This includes considering taxes, inflation, investments, spending habits, and more.

By taking a comprehensive approach to money management, individuals and businesses can ensure that their finances are in good health and that they are making the most of their money.

Smart money management is an important part of leading a prosperous life. It's all about understanding how to live within your means and make wise investments for the future.

With the right strategy and approach, you can create financial stability and security, no matter what your current situation is.

In this article, we'll explore the power of smart money management and provide you with the tools and resources to live well on a budget and invest wisely in your future.

THE FIVE PRINCIPLES OF MONEY

1. Spend less than you earn - This is a basic principle of personal finance. By spending less than you earn, you will be able to save and invest money for the future.

2. Pay yourself first - Start by setting aside a portion of your income each month to contribute to your savings or investments.

This will make it easier to save and invest in the future.

3. Have an emergency fund - This is important to ensure that you have a financial cushion in case of unexpected expenses or income loss.

4. Make a budget and stick to it - A budget will help you keep track of your income and expenses, and ensure that you are not spending more than you can afford.

5. Invest for the long-term - Investing for the long-term will help you maximize your returns over time and build wealth.

Smart money management is a powerful concept that can help you maximize your financial goals. It involves taking a proactive approach to budgeting and investing so that you can make informed decisions about how to use your money.

When done right, smart money management can help you save for retirement, pay off debt, and build wealth. Additionally, it can help you anticipate unexpected expenses and create a plan for achieving financial stability.

CHAPTER ONE

SETTING UP YOUR BUDGET

The key to wise money management is making and adhering to a budget. Having a budget will help you track your income, expenses, and savings and give you a better understanding of how to make the most of your finances.

It's important to assess your current financial situation, including your income, expenses, and any existing debts. Once you've taken a look at your current financial situation, you can begin setting up a budget.

The first step in creating your budget is to take a realistic inventory of your financial situation. You must figure out how much money you make each month and how much you spend each month. This includes utilities, insurance, loan payments, rent or mortgage payments, and other debts.

Create your budget once you are aware of your monthly income and expenses. To do this, make sure that you're living within your means and not spending more than you make.

Decide on your objectives first. Do you want to put money aside for retirement, debt repayment, or a down payment on a home? Determine how much you must set aside each month for savings after you have established your goals.

Making sure you budget for all essentials is the next stage. Establish a modest budget for food, transportation, entertainment, and other necessities first. Additionally, make sure to account for any contributions to savings in your budget.

It's critical to monitor your spending and adhere to your budget. Once you have your budget set up, it's important to track your progress. This will help you stay on budget and identify any areas where you may need to adjust your budget for more effective money management.

You can use cash to prevent overspending or set up automatic transfers to assist you in staying on target. Once you've created your budget, it's crucial to routinely examine it and, if required, make adjustments.

With careful budgeting, you may maximize your funds and accomplish your financial objectives.

Finally, it's important to invest in your future. This may include setting aside money for emergency savings, retirement, and other long-term financial goals. With good budgeting and smart money management, you can create a secure financial future.

1.1. UNDERSTANDING YOUR FINANCIAL SITUATION

Understanding your financial situation is a crucial step to managing your money and ensuring that you have a secure financial future. To gain a comprehensive understanding of your financial situation, you must evaluate your current income, assets, expenses, and debts.

Once you have this information, you can begin to make informed decisions about your finances and create a plan for your future.

The first step to understanding your financial situation is to track your income and expenses.

Create a budget that reflects your current financial situation and includes all of your income sources. Include all of your fixed expenses such as rent, car payments, and insurance, as well as variable expenses such as food and entertainment.

Record all of your expenses and income each month to get an accurate picture of your spending habits.

This can also help you identify areas where you could potentially reduce spending. Are you looking to save for retirement, invest, build an emergency fund, or do something else? Once you know where you want your funds to go, you can create a plan for where to put them every month.

It's important to remember that budgeting and investing is an ongoing processes, so it's important to review your plan regularly to make sure it's still appropriate for your goals.

Financial literacy is important because it helps you understand your current financial situation. This can help you make sound financial decisions and plan for the future. It can also help you identify financial risks and plan for potential pitfalls.

Knowing your financial situation can help you manage your money more effectively and achieve your financial goals.

FINANCIAL LITERACY

Financial literacy is important because it helps people understand how to make informed decisions about their money and gives them the power to make smart financial decisions.

Financial literacy teaches people how to budget, save, invest, and understand the basics of financial planning.

It also helps people to understand the different types of financial products, such as credit cards, mortgages, insurance, and investments.

With financial literacy, people can also learn about financial instruments, and how to interpret financial terms and statements.

Finally, financial literacy provides people with the knowledge and skills to help them with managing their money and achieve their financial goals.

RULES TO IMPROVE YOUR FINANCIAL SITUATION

1. Create a budget: Start by tracking your expenses and income. This will help you better understand your cash flow and

identify areas where you can make changes to save money.

2. Live Within Your Means: This means spending less than you make over time. You can do this by cutting back on expenses, increasing your income, or both.

3. Pay Off Debt: Start by targeting debts with the highest interest rates first. You may also want to consider a debt consolidation loan to lower your monthly payments.

4. Automatic Savings: Setting aside money each month for savings helps you prepare for unexpected expenses and build a financial cushion.

5. Plan for Retirement: It's never too early to start planning for retirement. Consider

meeting with a financial advisor to create a retirement plan that works for your unique situation.

6. Invest Wisely: Investing in the stock market can be a great way to grow your wealth over time. However, it's important to do your research and understand the risks before investing.

7. Get Insured: Having the right insurance coverage is essential to protecting your finances. Consider different types of insurance, such as life, health, auto, and home.

8. Build an Emergency Fund: Unexpected expenses like auto repairs or medical bills can put a strain on your budget. An emergency fund will help you cover these expenses without going into debt.

9. Take Advantage

ASSESSING YOUR FINANCIAL SITUATION

Assessing your financial situation is important for setting and achieving financial goals. To get a clear picture of your financial situation, you will need to track your income, expenses, and assets.

First, start by tracking your income. Record all sources of income, such as your salary, investments, and any other sources. Make sure to include all income, no matter how small.

Next, track your expenses. Record all your fixed and variable expenses. This includes rent, utility bills, food, entertainment, and any other payments.

Finally, calculate your net worth. This is the total value of all your assets, such as cash, investments, and property, minus your liabilities, such as student loans and credit card debt. Knowing your net worth will help you keep track of your financial progress.

Assessing your financial situation gives you a better understanding of your finances and allows you to set realistic goals. By tracking your income, expenses, and assets, you can make better decisions to improve your financial health.

1.2. ESTABLISHING FINANCIAL GOALS

Establishing financial goals is an important part of smart money management. Goals give you direction for your financial decisions, help motivate you to stay on track, and provide a reward when you've accomplished something.

When establishing financial goals, it's important to remember that financial goals are unique to each individual. What works for one person may not work for another. Set goals that you can realistically achieve and enjoy the process of reaching each goal.

The most important step in setting financial goals is to take time to plan. Figure out what you want to accomplish and how you will achieve it. Make sure your goals are SMART: Specific, Measurable, Achievable, Relevant, and Timely.

Before you start, consider your current financial situation. Look at your current income, expenses, and debt. This will give you an idea of what your starting point is and what you need to do to reach your financial goals.

Once you know your current financial situation and what you want to accomplish, you can start to set realistic goals.

Establish short-term goals that are easier to achieve and will give you immediate gratification. Then set long-term goals that will help you achieve financial freedom.

When setting financial goals, it's important to be diligent. Track your progress, review your goals often, and adjust them as needed. With the right attitude and the right plan, you can achieve all of them.

TYPES OF GOALS

SHORT-TERM GOALS
Short-term goals are objectives that you want to achieve within a short period,

usually in a matter of days, weeks, or months. Examples of short-term goals include:
• Saving up money for a car down payment
• Developing a budget
• Creating a savings plan
• Paying off credit card debt
• Building an emergency fund
• Improving credit score
• Achieving a higher savings rate
• Increasing net worth
• Reaching a specific level of income
• Establishing an investment portfolio
• Learning a new skill

LONG TERM GOALS

Long-term goals are those goals that you set for yourself to achieve in a longer period, usually over a year or more.

Examples of long-term goals include saving up to buy a house, starting a business, getting a degree, and traveling to a certain destination.

EXAMPLES OF FINANCIAL GOALS

A financial goal is an ambition or aspiration related to managing and growing your finances. Financial goals are typically long-term and can include things like saving for retirement, buying a house, or paying down debt.

You can break down your financial goals into short-term and long-term objectives to make them easier to track and reach.

Some examples of short-term financial goals may include saving money for a vacation, paying off one credit card balance, or contributing to an emergency fund.

Examples of long-term financial goals might include saving for retirement, paying off a mortgage, or eliminating debt.

Financial goals should be tailored to your individual needs and updated as your life and financial situation change.

Financial goals are important milestones to strive for when managing your money. Some of the most common financial goals include:

1. Creating an emergency fund: An emergency fund can provide financial security in times of difficulty. It serves as a way to pay for unexpected expenses, such as medical bills, car repairs, or job loss.

2. Paying off debt: Paying off debt can be a difficult, but rewarding financial goal. It involves making consistent, on-time payments to reduce the amount of debt you owe and eventually pay it off.

3. Saving for retirement: Saving for retirement is a long-term goal that requires dedication and consistency. The earlier you start saving, the more time your money will have to grow and accumulate.

4. Building financial independence: Financial independence is the ability to make money without relying on a steady paycheck. This could mean investing in stocks, bonds, or real estate. It could also mean starting a business or side hustle.

5. Establishing good credit: Good credit is a valuable asset that can help you save

money on loans and interest rates. Establishing good credit involves making payments on time and keeping your credit utilization low.

6. Investing: Investing is a great way to build wealth and secure your financial future. Investing involves putting money into stocks, bonds, mutual funds, or other securities that can generate returns over time.

COMPONENT OF FINANCIAL GOALS

Financial goals involve short-term and long-term objectives. Short-term goals may include saving for a down payment on a house, paying off credit card debt, or finding ways to reduce monthly living expenses.

Long-term goals may include retirement planning, saving for children's college tuition, or planning for major life events, such as a wedding or a home renovation.

The components of a financial goal include:

1. Setting a Goal: Decide what you want to accomplish financially, and make sure it's realistic and attainable.

2. Budgeting: Create a budget and track your spending so you know how much money you have available and where it's going.

3. Saving: Set aside money regularly to help you reach your financial goals.

4. Investing: Invest your money to help it grow over time.

5. Risk Management: Evaluate the risks associated with your investment strategy and adjust your plan accordingly.

6. Goal Evaluation: Check in on your progress and adjust your plan as needed to ensure you're staying on track.

GUIDELINES TO CREATE FINANCIAL GOALS

Financial goals are an important part of money management and should be taken seriously. When setting financial goals, it's important to be realistic and create achievable goals. To do this, break larger goals down into smaller, actionable steps and prioritize the ones that are most important to you. Here are some tips for setting financial goals:

1. Write down what you want to achieve. Your financial goals should be specific and measurable, so you can track your progress.

2. Set a timeline for each goal. Having a timeline for your goals will help you stay motivated and stay on track.

3. Create a budget. Having a budget will help you stay on top of your expenses and stay within your means.

4. Make a plan to reach your goals. Make sure you have a plan in place to reach your goals. This could include creating a savings plan, paying off debt, or investing.

5. Stay disciplined. Make sure you stick to your plan and stay disciplined. It will help you stay on track and reach your goals.

6. Re-evaluate and adjust as needed. Life happens and things can change. It's important to re-evaluate your goals and adjust them if needed.

By following these tips, you can create smart financial goals that will help you achieve your financial dreams.

STEP TO ACHIEVE YOUR GOAL

To achieve long and short-term goals, you will need to create a plan that outlines the steps you need to take to reach your goals. You will need to consider factors such as
• Timeline
• Budget
• Resources and resources available.
•You should also consider how you will measure your success.

Additionally, you should review your progress regularly to ensure that you are on track toward achieving your goals. Lastly, you should make sure that your goals are achievable and realistic.

1.3. CREATING A BUDGET

Creating a budget is an important step in developing a financial plan. It helps you track how much money you're bringing in, how much you're spending, and where your money is going.

To create a budget, you should start by tracking your income and expenses for a few months. Once you have a good understanding of your spending habits, you can start creating your budget.

Your budget should include all of your income, fixed expenses (such as rent or mortgage payments), and variable expenses (such as groceries or entertainment).

Once you have all of this information in one place, you can start setting goals and adjusting your spending to reach those goals.

With a budget in place, you'll be able to save money, reach your financial goals, and have better control of your money.

STEPS FOR CREATING A BUDGET

Creating a budget is essential for smart money management. It's a great way to stay on top of your finances and ensure that you're living within your means. To get started:

1. Gather all your financial information. This includes pay stubs, loan statements, and bank statements.

2. Make a list of all your income sources. This will help you determine how much money you have to work with each month.

3. Create a budget that includes all of your monthly expenses. Think of items like rent, utilities, groceries, and entertainment.

4. Set up a tracking system. This could be a spreadsheet or an app like Mint. Record all your expenses in this system so you can see how you're spending your money.

5. Stick to your budget and keep track of your progress. Review your budget and spending history periodically and make adjustments as needed.

Following these steps will help you become more financially savvy and ensure that you're managing your money smartly and responsibly.

1.4. TRACKING YOUR EXPENSES

Tracking your expenses is an important part of managing your finances. It helps you get a better understanding of how much money you're spending and where it's going.

The best way to track your expenses is to create a budget and stick to it. You can track your expenses by logging your expenses in a notebook or spreadsheet, or by using a budgeting app.

When tracking your expenses, make sure to include all types of expenses, such as bills, groceries, entertainment, and travel. Make sure to also track your income, so you can see how much money you're saving.

Finally, review your spending habits regularly to make sure you're staying on track and keeping your budget in check.

Tracking expenses is an important part of smart money management.
It's the process of tracking all your expenses, both large and small, so you can create a budget and manage your money more effectively.

By tracking your expenses, you can learn where your money is going and whether or not you're staying within your budget.

Tracking expenses can help you identify areas where you can save money, plan for big expenses, and adjust your spending habits to reach your financial goals.

To track your expenses, start by creating a list of all your monthly expenses, such as rent, utilities, groceries, and entertainment. Then, break down each expense into categories, such as travel and clothing.

Finally, track your expenses by writing down the amount you spend in each category every month.

You can also use budgeting software and apps to help you track your expenses. With the right tools, tracking your expenses can be simple and easy.

THE IMPORTANCE OF TRACKING YOUR EXPENSES

Tracking expenses is an essential part of smart money management. It helps you stay aware of how much money is coming in and going out, so you can make sure you are living within your means.

By tracking your expenses, you can also identify areas where you may be overspending and areas where you can save.

Keeping track of your expenses also helps you plan for long-term goals, such as saving for retirement or a down payment on a house. It also allows you to create and manage a budget, so that you can reach your financial goals and make the most of your hard-earned money.

KEYS TO KEEPING TRACK OF YOUR EXPENSES

Smart money management is key in keeping track of your expenses. One of the best ways to do this is by setting up a budget.

Figure out how much income you typically have, and then decide how you'll spend it.

 Break your spending down into categories like rent, groceries, entertainment, and more, and set limits for each. Write down all of your expenses, and keep track of them often.

You can also create a financial plan to help you stay on track. Outline your goals, both short-term and long-term, and how you plan to achieve them.

You can set milestones to review your progress and make adjustments accordingly.

Another option is to use budgeting and tracking apps to help you manage your expenses. Some apps, like Mint and Wally, provide detailed analysis of your spending habits and will alert you when you're close to exceeding your budget. These apps are great for visualizing your financial situation and helping you stay on top of your spending.

Overall, with the right tools and strategies, you can keep track of your expenses and better manage your finances. This can help you reach your financial goals and give you peace of mind.

CHAPTER TWO

STICKING TO A BUDGET

Sticking to a budget is one of the most powerful tools available to those looking to gain control over their finances and make the most of their money.

A budget is an effective way to set spending goals, prioritize goals, and track progress toward reaching them. Creating a budget and sticking to it can help to reduce stress, increase financial security, and reach financial goals.

The first step in creating a budget is to identify your income sources and track expenses. This will help you determine how much money you have to work with and how to best allocate it. Once your income and expenses have been established, you can set up a budget plan that will allow you to stay on track.

Setting short-term and long-term financial goals is another important part of sticking to a budget. Knowing what you want to save for and when you want to reach those goals can help to keep you motivated and on track. It can also help to keep you from overspending and creating more debt than necessary.

Making small, incremental changes to your budget is also a great way to stay on track. Small adjustments to your spending, such as cutting back on impulse purchases or meals out, can have a big impact on your budget.

It's also important to remember that sticking to a budget doesn't mean you can't enjoy life. It just means that you need to be mindful of your spending and prioritize your goals.

Sticking to a budget is key for smart money management. It helps to track your income and expenses and ensures that you are not overspending. Here are some tips for sticking to a budget:

1. Set realistic goals for your budget: It is important to set realistic goals that are attainable and that you can stick to.

2. Track your spending: This helps to keep you on track and ensures that you are not overspending.

3. Create a budget that is tailored to you: This can be done by looking at your current income and expenses and then creating a budget that works for you.

4. Make a plan: This plan should be tailored to your budget and should include short and long-term goals.

5. Automate your finances: Automating your finances can help you stick to your budget and ensure that your expenses are paid on time.

6. Make sure you have an emergency fund: This helps you to stay on track with your budget and ensures that you are prepared for unexpected expenses.

7. Stay motivated: Motivation is key for sticking to a budget and achieving your goals.

By following these tips, you can create a budget that works for you and stick to it.

This will help you achieve financial freedom and smart money management.

HOW TO CREATE A BUDGET

Creating a budget is an important step for managing your money smartly. It involves assessing your current financial situation, setting financial goals, and tracking your spending.

First, assess your current financial situation by gathering information about your income, expenses, assets, and debts. Calculate your net worth by subtracting your liabilities from your assets.

Second, set financial goals by identifying your short-term and long-term goals. These can include smaller goals like saving for a vacation or larger goals like saving for retirement.

Third, create a budget that works for you. Start by calculating your take-home pay, then subtract your fixed expenses like rent or mortgage payments and other bills. Once you have your variable expenses, like entertainment and eating out, you can determine how much you can spend on them.

Fourth, track your spending. Use a budgeting app or spreadsheet to help you keep track of how much you're spending and where. Make sure to review your budget regularly to make sure you're staying on track.

Creating a budget is a great way to manage your money smartly and stay on top of your finances. It will help you reach your financial goals and ensure you're staying on track.

2.1. UNDERSTANDING SELF-CONTROL AND SELF-IMPOSED LIMIT

Self-imposed limits and self-control are two important elements when it comes to smart money management.

Self-imposed limits refer to the limits that an individual sets for themselves, for example, setting a budget and a plan for their spending.

Self-control is the ability to delay gratification and to stay within those limits. Setting limits and practicing self-control helps to ensure that money is not wasted and that it is used wisely.

It is important to remember that self-imposed limits are not set in stone and can be adjusted, as long as they don't become too lax. Self-control is also essential, as it provides the discipline to stick to the limits that have been set.

Additionally, self-control allows individuals to make wise decisions when it comes to spending, investing, and saving money. By practicing self-control and having self-imposed limits, individuals can become smarter with their money and make better financial decisions.

SELF-IMPOSED LIMITS AND HOW TO OVERCOME THEM.

Self-imposed limits are limitations that we set for ourselves, and they often prevent us from achieving our full potential.

To overcome these self-imposed limits, it is important to recognize that they exist in the first place. Once they are identified, it is important to focus on the reasons why these limits were created and then work to find ways to break through them.

This could involve challenging negative beliefs, creating new goals, or seeking out resources and support to help reach those goals.

Additionally, it is important to practice self-compassion and to be kind to oneself when making mistakes or failing.

CONSEQUENCES OF LACK OF SELF-CONTROL FOR SMART MONEY MANAGEMENT

The lack of self-control when it comes to money management can lead to several consequences.

Without self-discipline, it can be difficult to save money, stick to a budget, and make wise financial decisions. As a result, one may find themselves in debt, with no emergency fund, and a lack of financial security.
In addition, an inability to control spending can lead to impulse purchases and an accumulation of unnecessary items. This can lead to an increase in stress, financial anxiety, and an overall decrease in quality of life.

It is essential to practice self-control when it comes to managing your finances. It is important to set clear goals, create a budget, stay organized, and always be aware of how you are spending your money. Taking control of your finances can lead to a more secure future, better financial habits, and an improved quality of life.

2.2 MAKING A SMART CHOICE

Making smart choices when it comes to finances is a must to protect your financial security and reach your financial goals.

Being smart about your money means understanding your options before making a decision. It also means understanding the risks involved in any decision you make.

Before you make any financial decision, it's important to understand all of your options, the potential risks and rewards, and any applicable fees. Doing research ahead of time can help you make a smart decision and avoid making a costly mistakes.

Take the time to review your finances regularly and plan for the future. This includes understanding your income and expenses and setting financial goals. Implementing a budget and tracking your spending can help you stay on track and reach your financial goals.

If you're considering a loan, credit card, or any other type of financing, research the terms and conditions carefully. Make sure you understand all of the associated costs and fees and compare several options before making a decision.

Finally, it's important to remember that there is no one-size-fits-all approach to making smart financial decisions. It's important to do your research and make decisions that are right for you and your financial situation.

Making smart money choices is a key component of smart money management. Having a clear understanding of your financial goals, and creating a budget, can help you make informed decisions that will help you reach those goals.

To start, it's important to assess your current financial situation. Track your income, expenses, and debts, and create a list of your financial goals and priorities.

Once you have a better idea of your current financial situation, you'll be ready to make smarter financial decisions. Creating a budget is an important step in this process.

A budget can help you track and manage your finances, and ensure that you are not spending more than you can afford. Additionally, setting limits on your spending can help you avoid unnecessary debt.

Making smart money choices also means investing money wisely. Prioritize your financial goals and create a plan to reach them.

Consider using tax-advantaged accounts, such as individual retirement accounts (IRAs) and 401(k) plans, to help you reach your retirement savings goals.

Research and compare different investments, such as stocks, mutual funds, and bonds, to determine which ones are best suited to your financial objectives.

Finally, make sure to stay informed about the changing financial landscape. Keep up with news and developments in the financial markets, and consider consulting a financial advisor if necessary.

A financial professional can help you make better decisions and provide guidance in the often-complicated world of finance.

SMART-MONEY HABITS

Smart money management is essential for achieving financial goals and creating a secure future. Here are a few smart money habits that can help:

1. Budget: Creating and sticking to a budget is the most important money habit. It helps you prioritize spending, save on unnecessary expenses, and achieve financial goals.

2. Save: Make saving a priority by setting aside a certain amount each month for savings or investments. This can help you

build an emergency fund and create financial security.

3. Track expenses: Tracking expenses helps you identify areas where you can save money and make changes to your budget.

4. Spend wisely: Spending money wisely is essential for managing your money. Try to make purchases that are within your means and that will add value to your life.

5. Research: Researching different financial products like credit cards, loans, and investments can help you make informed decisions.

6. Plan: Creating a plan for achieving your financial goals can help you stay focused and motivated.

By incorporating these smart money habits into your lifestyle, you can take control of your finances and create a secure future.

HOW TO MAKE SMART FINANCIAL CHOICES

Making smart financial choices starts with understanding where your money is coming from and going.

Begin by creating a budget that tracks your income and expenses. Make sure to include fixed costs, such as rent or mortgage payments, and variable costs, such as gas for your car.

Consider the difference between your needs (like food and housing) and your wants (like travel and entertainment). Use your budget to help prioritize your spending and determine how much money you can put toward savings and investments.

Once you have an understanding of your income and expenses, create a plan to start saving.

Set aside a certain amount every month that can be used to meet your financial goals like paying down debt, building an emergency fund, or saving for retirement. Consider setting up automatic transfers to ensure that your savings are taken care of each month.

In addition to saving, you should also consider investments. Before investing, it's important to make sure you understand the different types of investments, their risks, and potential returns.

You should also understand the tax implications of any investments you make. A financial advisor can help you evaluate your situation and recommend an appropriate strategy.

Finally, it's important to stay informed and educated about the financial markets to make informed decisions. Keeping up with the news and connecting with financial professionals can help you stay up to date on the latest trends and strategies. By following these tips, you can make smart financial choices for your future.

2.3. AVOIDING UNNECESSARY SPENDING

Smart money management is vital for achieving financial security, and avoiding unnecessary spending is a key part of that.

It can be hard to resist the lure of impulse buys or even pricey items when you have the means to afford them. But, it is important to remember that the money you spend today could have been better invested for long-term financial success.

To avoid unnecessary spending, start by setting a budget and tracking your spending. This will help you identify where you can make cuts and ensure that you are staying within your budget.

Additionally, it can be helpful to create a list of items you want to buy, and wait at least a week before making the purchase.

This will give you the time to research the item and make an informed decision about whether or not it is a necessity. Finally, you can use cash instead of a credit card to help you stay within your budget.

By following these steps you can avoid unnecessary spending and develop smart money management habits. This will create a strong financial foundation and help you attain your financial goals.

2.4 DON'T GIVE UP

Never give up on the power of smart money management. It may seem daunting at first, but having a sound strategy for managing your finances can have a positive impact on your life.

Taking the time to properly plan and manage your finances can help you achieve your financial goals, such as saving for retirement, paying off debt, or investing in the stock market.

By being proactive about your finances, you can gain the confidence you need to make sound financial decisions and be in control of your finances.

Some key steps to smart money management include developing a budget, creating an emergency fund, setting financial goals, and tracking your expenses.

A budget is a great way to keep track of your income and expenses, so you know how much money you have available to save and invest.

An emergency fund can help cushion the blow of unexpected expenses, such as medical bills or car repairs. Setting financial goals will help you stay on track and motivated to reach your desired outcome.

Finally, tracking your expenses will help you stay within your budget and identify areas where you are overspending.

Smart money management is often easier said than done, but it is possible. By committing to a plan and following through, you can achieve your financial goals and gain financial freedom.

Smart money management is essential to achieving financial success. No matter how tough life can get, don't give up on planning and saving for your future.

Being able to manage your money smartly involves creating a budget, setting financial goals, and tracking expenses. It also means recognizing when you need to make adjustments to stay on track.

Have a plan for saving and investing, and be sure to make regular contributions towards these goals. The more you can stay disciplined and follow your plan, the more likely you are to reach your financial objectives.

Don't give up on smart money management, even when it may feel impossible to stay on track. You can make smart financial decisions that will get you closer to your goals.

CHAPTER THREE

INVEST WISELY

Investing wisely involves making informed decisions with your financial resources. It involves thoroughly researching different investment strategies and exploring various options to ensure you're making the best decisions for your financial future.

When investing, it's important to understand your risk tolerance and invest only in products and services that you understand and are comfortable with.

You should also diversify your investments across different asset classes to reduce the risk of losing your entire investment.

Additionally, it's important to regularly monitor your investments and update them as your financial goals and risk tolerance change.

Investing wisely involves more than just picking stocks, bonds, and other financial products.

It's about having a long-term plan that helps you make sound decisions and manage your money effectively.

Smart money management can help you reach your financial goals, save for the future, and make the most of your resources. Here are some tips on investing wisely:

1. Start by setting specific goals. Before you start investing, determine what you want to achieve with your money. Are you hoping to grow your wealth, save for retirement, or buy a house? Determining your goals will help you decide which investments are best for you.

2. Research investments carefully. Don't rush into investing without doing your research. Take the time to understand the various types of investments available, and determine which ones are right for you. Consider the risks, fees, and returns of each option before committing your money.

3. Diversify your investments. Don't put all your eggs in one basket. Spreading your investments across different asset classes can help reduce risk while potentially increasing returns over time.

4. Consider your investment horizon. How long do you plan to invest your money? Think about how much time you have to invest and how much risk you are willing to take.

5. Develop a disciplined investing strategy. Sticking to a consistent plan is key to long-term investing success. Establish a schedule for regular contributions, and decide which investments you

THREE BEST INVESTMENT

The three best investments for increasing your wealth are :
Stocks
Bonds
Real estate.
Stocks offer the potential for long-term growth,
Bonds offer a stable income stream and a measure of safety, and real estate can provide both income and appreciation. Each of these investments has its unique

advantages and risks, so it is important to research each one to determine which is best for your needs.

PRINCIPLE TO GET AN EARLY START ON INVESTING WISELY

1. Set Clear Goals: Figure out why you want to invest and what you want to get out of it.

2. Understand Risk: Understand the risks associated with investing and how to manage them.

3. Choose the Right Account: Decide which account types are best for you and which will help you reach your goals.

4. Research Your Investments: Research your potential investments before committing your money to them.

5. Start Small: Start with small amounts and gradually increase your investments as you gain more knowledge and experience.

6. Rebalance Regularly: Make sure your investments remain aligned with your goals by conducting regular rebalancing.

TIPS FOR INVESTING WISELY

Here are some tips for investing wisely:
1. Start early: The sooner you start investing, the more time you have to benefit from compound interest.

2. Diversify your investments: Don't put all your eggs in one basket; diversifying your investments can help reduce risk.

3. Understand your investment choices: Research and understand the various investment options available and their associated risks.

4. Create a plan and stick with it: Create a plan that takes into account your goals, risk tolerance, and timeline.

5. Monitor your investments: Stay informed and monitor your investments regularly to ensure they're performing as expected.

3.1. EVALUATING INVESTMENT OPPORTUNITY

Evaluating investment opportunities is a critical part of smart money management. Smart money management involves taking calculated risks and assessing the potential returns of each investment option.

It also requires considering factors such as the amount of risk associated with each option, the liquidity of the investment, and the fees associated with investing.

When evaluating investment opportunities, investors must consider not only the potential gains but also the potential losses and the time frame for the investment.

Investors must also consider the overall market conditions and the current economic climate to identify potential areas of opportunity.

Additionally, investors must analyze the underlying fundamentals of the security, such as its financial health, management team, and competitive landscape to make a wise investment decision.

Finally, investors must consider their personal goals and objectives, such as their desired timeline for the investment and their risk tolerance, to ensure that the investment aligns with their financial needs.

By evaluating investment opportunities thoughtfully and thoroughly, investors can maximize their returns while minimizing their risks. This is the power of smart money management.

CHECKLIST TO EVALUATE THE POTENTIAL OF AN INVESTMENT

1. Analyze the current and projected financial performance of the investment.
2. Determine the investment's risk profile.
3. Assess the liquidity of the investment.
4. Analyze the current and projected competitive environment.
5. Review the management team and their track record.
6. Analyze the current and projected regulations that may affect the investment.
7. Consider the potential return on the investment.
8. Examine the potential tax implications of the investment.
9. Consider the potential for asset diversification.

10. Analyze the potential for future capital appreciation.

METHODS FOR EVALUATING CAPITAL INVESTMENT PROPOSAL

Evaluating a capital investment proposal is an important part of the decision-making process. It involves analyzing the potential benefits and risks associated with the proposed project, as well as its overall financial feasibility. The most common methods used to evaluate capital investment proposals include

The Net Present Value (NPV) method
The Internal Rate of Return (IRR) method, the Payback Period method, and the Capital Budgeting process.

The Net Present Value method calculates the present value of future cash flows associated with the investment proposal. It takes into account the time value of money, as well as inflation.

The Internal Rate of Return method measures the rate of return on the proposed investment, taking into account all associated costs and benefits. The Payback Period method calculates the amount of time it will take to recover the initial investment.

Finally, the Capital Budgeting process is a comprehensive process that involves estimating the cash flows associated with the project, assessing the associated risks, and assessing the overall financial feasibility of the project.

3.2 AVOIDING SCAM

The power of smart money management can help you avoid scams. Scams can take many forms, from fake investments to online phishing and identity theft. Being aware of the different types of scams and taking steps to protect yourself can help you avoid falling victim to one.

First and foremost, do your research. Don't fall for get-rich-quick schemes or any offers that seem too good to be true. Research the company, its background, and any reviews or customer feedback to determine if it is legitimate. Be wary of any requests for personal information or money.

When in doubt, trust your gut. If something feels suspicious or wrong, it's best to stay away. Even if the offer seems legitimate, it's still best to do your due diligence.

You should also be wary of any unfamiliar emails or phone calls. Don't click on any suspicious links, and don't give out personal information to anyone you don't know.

Finally, be sure to keep your information secure and up-to-date. Make sure you have strong passwords for all of your accounts and be sure to change them regularly. Make sure to keep a backup of all your important documents, and store them in a safe place.

By following these simple steps, you can avoid becoming a victim of scams and better protect your finances.

It is important to be aware of scams so that you can protect yourself and your finances. Here are some ways to avoid scams:

1. Research before you invest: Make sure to do your due diligence and research any investment opportunity or individual offering you a financial deal.

2. Verify the legitimacy of websites and emails: Don't click on links within emails or online ads unless you are sure they are legitimate.

3. Don't share personal information: Never share personal information such as your bank account number, Social Security number, or passwords with anyone.

4. Don't respond to phone calls or emails: If you receive a phone call or email offering financial services, do not respond.

5. Double-check sources: If you're offered a financial opportunity, double-check the source. Ask friends and family for advice.

6. Ask questions: If you have any doubts or suspicions about a deal, ask questions and get answers.

7. Don't pay upfront fees: Be aware of any companies or individuals asking for an upfront fee before providing services.

8. Be cautious of "too good to be true" deals: Do not believe any offers that seem too good to be true.

9. Report suspicious activity: If you suspect that you have been a victim of a financial scam, report it to the authorities.

WAYS TO AVOID INVESTMENT

Scams can come in many different forms and can target anyone, regardless of age or income level. To help protect yourself from scams, keep the following in mind:

• Do your research: Research any company or individual you plan to do business with before committing.

• Watch for red flags: Be wary of anyone who insists on an immediate payment or asks for sensitive information such as your Social Security number or bank account number without verifying your identity.

• Don't fall for pressure tactics: Resist any pressure to act quickly, especially if they say the offer is time-sensitive or limited.

• Don't pay upfront fees: Legitimate companies typically don't ask for money upfront.

• Stay alert: Be on the lookout for anything that looks suspicious or seems too good to be true. If something doesn't feel right, trust your instinct and don't proceed with the transaction.

3.3. CREATING A PORTFOLIO

Creating a portfolio is a process of selecting investments that match your investing goals, timeline, and risk tolerance.

It is important to consider a variety of factors when creating a portfolio such as an asset allocation, diversification, and the expected return on investment.

To start, you should determine your goals, timeline, and risk tolerance.

Next, you should decide on the asset allocation for your portfolio. Asset allocation is the process of allocating your funds across different asset classes such as stocks, bonds, and cash.

After you decide on your asset allocation, you should diversify your portfolio by investing in different types of investments within each asset class.

Finally, you should determine the expected return on investment for each of your investments. With this information, you can create a portfolio that is tailored to your investing goals.

Creating a portfolio for smart money management is a great way to ensure that your money is working for you.

A portfolio is a selection of various investments that you have chosen to meet your financial goals. When building a portfolio, it is important to consider your risk tolerance and financial goals. You should also consider various asset classes and research different investments.

Once you have identified your financial goals and chosen your investments, you should then create a plan to monitor your portfolio's performance and make any adjustments if necessary. It is important to regularly analyze your portfolio and make sure that you are on track with your financial goals. You can also talk to a financial advisor if you need help.

Finally, make sure to stay up to date on the current financial and economic news and trends. You should also periodically review your investments and make sure that you are taking advantage of any new opportunities that may arise.

Smart money management is key to achieving your financial goals and creating a portfolio is one of the ways to do so.

HOW TO CREATE A PORTFOLIO

Creating a portfolio involves deciding which investments meet your financial goals, understanding the risks, and diversifying your holdings across different asset classes.

To begin, you should determine your financial goals, such as saving for retirement, buying a home, or funding your children's education.

You should also analyze your risk tolerance and determine your risk profile. This will help you form a portfolio that is in line with your goals and risk tolerance.

Once you have a plan, you can start building your portfolio by selecting investments that meet your objectives.

Consider diversifying your holdings to reduce risk, and make sure to research each investment before committing. You should also make sure to regularly monitor and rebalance your portfolio to ensure that it is staying aligned with your goals.

CREATING A PLAN TO MONITOR THE PORTFOLIO

Creating a plan to monitor a portfolio is essential to ensure that risks are minimized and goals are achieved.

The first step is to determine the type of portfolio that you want to monitor. Are you looking for a growth portfolio or a balanced portfolio? Depending on the type of portfolio, the goals and objectives of the portfolio should be identified.

Once the goals and objectives are determined, risk tolerance should be established. Risk tolerance is the amount of risk an investor is willing to take on to achieve their financial goals. This should be taken into account when selecting investments for the portfolio.

Next, the assets for the portfolio should be selected. Typically, this is done by researching investments that align with the goals and objectives of the portfolio and the investor's risk tolerance.

After the assets have been selected, the performance of the portfolio should be monitored regularly. This is done by tracking the performance of the assets in the portfolio.

Finally, the portfolio should be adjusted as needed. This means that the assets should be rebalanced if the performance of the assets deviates from the investor's goals and objectives. Rebalancing is done by increasing or decreasing the number of certain assets in the portfolio.

By creating a plan to monitor a portfolio, investors can ensure that their portfolio is performing as expected and that their financial goals are being met.

REVIEWING YOUR INVESTMENT

Reviewing your investments is an important part of managing your finances.

It helps you to assess the performance of your investments, identify any changes that need to be made, and ensure that your portfolio is on track to meet your goals.

When reviewing your investments, it is important to start with a review of your overall financial situation. This includes looking at your income, expenses, and any debt that you may have. It is also important to review your investment portfolio to make sure you are aware of all your assets, as well as any potential risks or rewards associated with them.

Once you have a good understanding of your overall financial situation, you can begin to review your investments. Evaluate your returns, review your asset allocation, and look for any opportunities to diversify your investments.

You can also review any fees or expenses associated with your investments so that you are aware of exactly what you're paying for.

Finally, make sure you are regularly monitoring your investments. This includes staying up-to-date on market news and trends, as well as checking in with your financial advisors or brokers.

The regular review helps you to stay on top of any changes to your investments, and to make timely decisions that can help you to reach your goals.

3.4. DIVERSIFYING YOUR INVESTMENT

Diversifying your investments is a smart way to manage your money and make sure that you are not putting all of your eggs in one basket.

By diversifying, you are spreading your investment across different types of assets, such as stocks, bonds, mutual funds, real estate, and commodities. This way, if one type of asset fails, the other types may still be performing well and can help to offset any losses.

Additionally, diversifying your investments can help to reduce overall risk and create a more balanced portfolio.

It is important to note that diversifying does not guarantee losses and should be done in conjunction with proper research and financial planning.

Diversifying your investment portfolio is an important strategy for managing risk and increasing the potential for higher returns.

Diversification involves spreading your investments across different asset classes, such as stocks, bonds, and real estate, as well as across different sectors and companies.

When constructing a diversified portfolio, it is important to consider the amount of risk you are willing to take, your investment goals, and the time horizon for achieving those goals.

A diversified portfolio may also include investments in commodities or alternative asset classes, such as derivatives or hedge funds.

By diversifying your investments, you can reduce the risk of losses that may be associated with any one asset class or sector, while still increasing your potential for higher returns over

BENEFITS OF DIVERSIFICATION

Diversification is a key concept in investing, and investors need to understand why it is so important.

Diversification is the practice of spreading out investments across different asset classes, or different types of investments, and is an important part of any portfolio. The main benefits of diversification include

Reducing risk and increasing returns. When an investor diversifies their portfolio, they are reducing their risk of suffering a significant loss in any one area. By spreading out investments across different asset classes, any losses in one area can be offset by gains in another area. This reduces the overall risk of the portfolio and can help protect investors from significant losses if the market turns against them.

Another benefit of diversification is that it can also increase returns. By investing in different asset classes, an investor can potentially benefit from the higher returns that come with different types of investments. This can help an investor maximize their returns, potentially leading to greater profits over the long run.

In summary, diversification is a key concept for any investor to understand. By diversifying their investments across different asset classes, investors can reduce their risk and potentially increase their returns. This can help investors protect their portfolios from market downturns, while also helping them maximize their profits in the long run.

STRATEGIES FOR DIVERSIFICATION OF INVESTMENT

Diversifying your investments is an important part of any successful financial plan.

Diversification is the process of spreading your investments across different asset classes, such as stocks, bonds, mutual funds, real estate, and cash and geographies.

This strategy helps to minimize risk and maximize returns. Examples of diversifying your investments include investing in stocks from different sectors to spread out your stock exposure; investing in government bonds to reduce volatility; investing in mutual funds to gain exposure to a variety of underlying investments; investing in real estate to gain exposure to a more tangible asset;

and keeping some of your assets in cash to provide liquidity.

By diversifying your investments, you can ensure that you will have a more balanced portfolio and reduce the risk of any single investment having a significant impact on your overall financial picture.

Additionally, you should consider investing in different types of financial instruments, such as stocks, bonds, mutual funds, ETFs, and other options. Lastly, you should also consider diversifying across different types of accounts, such as traditional, Roth, and SEP account

THE CONCLUSION

The power of smart money management is becoming increasingly important in today's world.

It can help individuals achieve their financial goals, manage their expenses and investments more effectively, and avoid costly mistakes.

With a little knowledge and practice, anyone can become a financial expert and be in control of their destiny.

Smart money management can be the difference between financial security and financial disaster.

Smart money management is the practice of taking control of finances by setting short- and long-term financial goals, budgeting, and tracking expenses creating a savings plan, and working to reduce debt.

It also involves taking advantage of financial resources and services, such as tax deductions, banking products, and investment options.

Smart money management helps individuals and families build wealth, achieve financial security and reach their financial goals.

The power of smart money management can be summed up in two words: budgeting and investing. By sticking to a budget and investing wisely, you can live well today and prepare for a secure financial fortune. By taking control of your finances, you can enjoy peace of mind now and a bright future ahead.

www.ingramcontent.com/pod-product-compliance
Lightning Source LLC
Chambersburg PA
CBHW070320220526
45465CB00013B/1499